Well-travelled, a user of the human condition. Witnessed globalisation, injustice, freedom, tyranny, peace, not war, communism, democracy, gentle and violent emotions, nihilism, cynicism.

To my sweetest critics, Aaron and Hannah.

Adrian Armanca

CHANCE AND LIFE

AUSTIN MACAULEY PUBLISHERS™

LONDON • CAMBRIDGE • NEW YORK • SHARJAH

A CIP catalogue record for this title is available from the British Library.

ISBN 9781398470132 (Paperback)
ISBN 9781398470149 (Hardback)
ISBN 9781398470156 (ePub e-book)

www.austinmacauley.com

First Published 2023
Austin Macauley Publishers Ltd®
1 Canada Square
Canary Wharf
London
E14 5AA

Chance

He ran away without a word
Reason being what he heard,
From them fosters, a hostile bunch
Berating him to cool their grudge.

Winter was approaching fast
With his bare feet, shirt small and tight,
The pants too short had nothing else
Since last year when he left the house.

Digging deep, diving head down
In some dumpster near a town,
Rummaging through scrape and waste
Buried halfway to his waist.

He found a box with glossy letters
Revealed to have few little treasures,
The world became his favourite place
Joyful mien filled his face.

Inside were shoes with polished leather
Never seen the rainy weather,
A pair of pants not sparse at knees
Not holey jacket like Swiss cheese.

One of the pockets had a note
Chilling, terrifying text it wrote,
Few words following his name
'Rest in peace, your soul we claim.'

A vacuous smile blew into laugh
Gargling sounds turned into cough,
Shots of blood went through his eyes
He died knowing his shoes were nice.

Sad Chance

Down on luck, out on the street
Nothing to wear, nor drink or eat,
He ran away while just a child
Then altered into something wild.

Drunk with freedom and sedated
Tranquillized and opiated,
Not seldom he will get his hit
Through petty crime, cheat and deceit.

He had good friends, people to love
In just a blink, ripped them all off,
He spoke few words and they were lies
Using his wit to get his "prize".

He died alone, they found him rotting
Left arm had the syringe still hanging,
He left a note to blame the world
Written while he overdosed.

His legacy was just a feeling
A rush to just forget his being,
Punished just for showing weakness
Brutal sentence? Well, we're humans!

Thin as Lines

Stretching lines and rays of light
From one side to the end of sight,
Following through bush and land
Covered with red dust and sand.

Immense, limitless, and vast
Fathom? Try not, your days won't last,
Can you attach a size or measure?
It can be done, will happen never!

Heedful with others, proud of traditions
Docile in nature, respecting its creatures,
The first-ever humans to visit these lands
Got rid of the future, took fate in their hands.

They were able to perceive the space
With only few senses humans possess,
Have tried in vain, the time to subdue
Endlessly seeking, still had not a clue.

Immured by the waters, far from the rest
Lands full of richness, nature has blessed,
Where there is a story for everything seen
Expressed as a painting with dots in between.

Patriotic

Enrolled, attired, and prepared
Promised everything he dreamed,
In exchange for taking lives
The more the better in their eyes.

Loaded in a big-black plane
Early dawn with heavy rain,
Men, a hundred with their guns
Someone's brothers, fathers and sons.

The sky still blue, earth dark below
A strange deep quiet started to grow,
Though engines roared, soldiers were chatting
An odd and tragic sense was floating.

Above some land with eerie name
Ghostly shadows traced with flame,
High and beyond with speeds of light
Burning everything in sight.

I saw their faces flush
While the sun began to blush,
Pushing rays through oval frames
Drawing auras on their shapes.

The fate was stamped onto their eyes
That sparkling shine it was demise,
Short clicks, brief silence, blast then flames
He pulled the pins of few grenades.

Not long before the sun has risen,
Ink was loaded, words were written,
The story of a hundred souls
Lost above some creepy holes.

Jack (Not the Ripper)

Streetlight
So bright
Metal glister
So sinister.

Short wait
Killer's trait
Call girl fit
Shiny blade hit.

Instant demise
His second prize
For the night
Under the same light.

Knife slash
Blood gush
Only thrill
Before the kill.

Always free
Died 93
Paying back?
Not for Jack.

After Pangea

A massive force splitting the land
Two hundred million years behind,
Rifts and fractures through the Earth
A new planet was given birth.

Life was sparse most went extinct
The nature purging without guilt,
No eyes to see what happened then
If not for luck would be the end.

What made it drift away from waning
A slow and self-destructive heading,
Was not the destiny, god, or creation
Was not the devil or the Satan.

It was nature that has failed
The fatal path it chose to trail,
Failed the atoms settlement
Its only botched experiment.

Humans, spoiled destructive species
A lump of protoplasm and faeces,
Putrid pots and leaking vessels
Nothing but skin covered barrels.

Greta chose to join the botching
The epicanthic Swedish something,
She wants vengeance against nature
"How dare you" messing with my future.

Let's save the putrid leaking vessels
Let's save these ugly covered barrels,
She thinks that nature will survive
While keeping these rodents alive?

Real

Vivid dream
A light beam
Flashing away
Across the bay.

The shadow inline
It was mine
Walking slow
Away from the glow.

My legs dropped
Being chopped
Shining in light
Meters apart.

Slender and tall
A wooden doll
Raised from the sand
Missing a hand.

I saw it chew
It was a shoe
Swallowing whole
With leg and all.

It belongs to me
The calf and the knee
A tendon still hangs
Between his long fangs.

Waking from terror
My body in tremor
Saw both shoes in pair
Next to my wheelchair.

Living With Deaf

Grab the cat!
I'm not fat.
Home soon,
Cruise to Cancún?

I'm off to bed
No, red instead
I'm fed up
Sure, I cleaned up.

Four times a day
Tenfold I say
Same thing again
Multiplied by ten.

Heedless and deaf
Who is that Jeff?
Oh God, march away
Really? Jeff's gay?

Today I chose to die
Not your hair but I
Thirty years of that
Where is the cat?

Forgive

A rainy day
His thoughts away,
Wounds still raw
Healing was slow.

A note she wrote
Left it afloat,
Washed away
It's what they say.

A month went by
His eyes were dry,
A call early dawn
They found her alone.

The note she left
Said it was a jest,
The man was his friend
She did put an end.

He did have forgiveness
Was more of a weakness,
Not long before
She walked out the door.

Again, lost her way
She came back that day,
She found him entangled
She also was troubled.

All three found a way
They couldn't say nay,
Laid and entwined
Top, front, or behind.

Tight

Curt in answers, blunt, and cruel
Ugly, stubborn as a mule,
His pockets only filled with cents
A dollar was a life expense.

Consumptive, riddled with disease
A life with him, she was Louise,
Reduced from years to only days
Not dying, living were her fears.

He left her there, before goodbyes
She is no good now that she dies,
In his mind was only fair
Was better anywhere but there.

Politics

Figure that
The world is flat
No inspiration left
Our brains are messed.

Few raised to show
The wit is so low
No need to think
Just water to drink.

Don't pollute the air
Your extras, do share
Pansexual or gay,
Not my problem, hey!

Internal combustion?
They stopped the production
Electric and solar
The world is bipolar.

'Yellow, black, or fat'
Can't use in a chat
Words like 'white'
Will set you alight.

World has gone nuts
Soon, hermaphrodites.
Wanna spawn?
You're on your own.

Great Fun

Words full of splendour,
Of love, sweet and tender
A bunch of daisies
Roses and lilies.

Marriage shortly trailed
Love has prevailed
Kids, soon to arrive
All three by surprise.

She's blonde with blue eyes
I'm white, eyes like skies
Last of them three
Dark brown like a tea.

What have you done?
Mbutu from Sudan?
Is he the donner?
The one with the bonner?

The rest? One's just like you
Not sure which of the two
I swear you are the one
The others? Just for fun.

I think is only fair
While standing on the chair
At least to kick it in
A rope below my chin.

All French

Paris, with its shops and parlours
With its arcades, bridges, towers
Victuals for every comer
Made to cure all types of hunger.

Haussmann's buildings raised in pair
Secrets, stories, tales they bear
Covered up with mystery
Heavy, rich in history.

One of yesterday's dark crimes
Managed to blemish our times
Paris from its Jewish quarter
'Human life' biggest exporter.

'Tabula rasa' a new beginning
Benign era, hoping and dreaming
Transient? Could be protracted.
Cruel past? Never reenacted.

Freedom

Yelling voices in my head
Pack your bags and run, they said,
Bow to freedom not to laws
Rebel, revolt for its cause.

Found myself free like a bird
Yelling voices? Not a word,
Vagabond through half the planet
Suddenly my dreams have vanished.

I needed meaning, not illusions
I needed questions, not solutions,
Valour could describe me then
Grasping my old life again.

Short-lived joy, until the pain
From my head, inside my brain,
It was a lump, size doesn't matter
Will kill me in a month not later.

I dealt with it, in virtue's way
By giving up, dying that day,
Got rid of freedom with my hand
Even the word I couldn't stand.

Comet

Red and yellow, livid rays
Has split the light in hundred ways,
The sun has shown its angry gaze
First time ever seen such blaze.

Oven hot, never before
Somewhere on the north seashore,
Midwinter or shortly thereafter
Nature forging a disaster.

Still calm, nothing has happened yet
Suddenly the sun has set,
A few hours earlier that day
The skies from blue turned into grey.

A freezing cold covered the bay
Not long after the skies turned grey,
So cold, was never felt before
Myriad dead birds on the shore.

Their corps were falling from the sky
Frozen wings bar them to fly,
Foaming sea freezing its waves
Eerie sight of dunes and caves.

Earth has lost its orbit course
A comet pushing with brute force,
That's it, so instant, trivial
Few stray lost rocks, vestigial.

Twins

Early morning, sudden clamour
Doors were shutting, sliding rubber,
Metal clacking, guns were loading
Voices yelling, knocks and stomping.

Half a dozen of them nazis
Young and pompous in their twenties,
Charging through the doors and stairs
Breaking tables, pushing chairs.

Wasn't a dream, it seemed so real
Started to question things that I feel,
"All night, the tv was on," she revealed
"Was also the wine and smoking the weed."

"Falling asleep on top of me,
Burping the sausage while finding my G,
Snoring and coughing, your tongue in my mouth
It was so romantic when shoved it down south."

Sophistry

The type who's digging deep for gold
Family, friends, everyone sold,
Hubris was her only trait
She hooked him while licking her bait.

Blue-blooded, haired like blushing sun
Small-beady eyes, vapid yet fun,
He believed her when she said
"The Earth is round, looks like your head."

The hook was: "Harry, shall we marry?
I think your baby's what I carry."
So that wasn't a girth of jelly?
Not even a big fat pot belly?

Not long ago you were romantic
Everything was slow and tantric,
You said I'm fine like bacon rind
You even had me from behind.

I loved the way you called me hoe
Looking at me like I'm a crow,
You only hit me once with love
Only nine teeth I've gotten rid of.

Leave the kingdom, be a traitor
Let's move in my white-trash trailer,
I'll be your trull loose and salacious
Guess what? I also have a penis.

I won't tell that you STD's
While flared up they ooze like cheese,
I won't tell that your uncle's brother
Might be a chance that is your father.

All Rich

'Listen,' he yelled, the crowd just stopped
Deep din of voices, all of them dropped,
He had the power to convince
Since just a child and ever since.

Growing up, he had a dream
To rule the world, the highest deem,
Then settled for a clerk position
Arousing his latest ambition.

Money, he counted until one day
Found himself entwined, to his dismay,
A plot, masterplan epic and hefty
Lifted his richness by millions, twenty.

Restless, pursuing his dream of control
Mazumas were flowing, not his only goal,
Employing by hundreds, youths with a vengeance
Oblivious, not knowing it was their sentence.

Not even a year, a hundred-fold richer
Tabloids depicted him as a debaucher,
Sniffing around it started to leak
Falling from grace in less than a week.

Only served time less than a day
Expired, they found his corps in decay,
He had a deep secret, he was condemned
I guess that's the story, we won't know the end.

Stalingrad

August day, a dewy morning
Chirping birds, by hundreds perching,
A gentle breeze whispering rhymes
Clouds in the sky drawing the signs.

No one could read or hear what they said
No one could see what happens ahead,
Some thought of slumber, a lazy Sunday
Others waiting for the greys of Monday.

He never comes on days like this
When sun is up, sending his bliss,
The faithful envoy bearing news
"All folks will have to pay their dues."

Monday, dawn, crammed with men
Murmur of voices saying amen,
Outside the trains, sadness and cries
Faces of loved ones saying their goodbyes.

Off to the lands of war and hatred
Lands with no reasons where violence is sacred,
Human life swapped for booty and loot
Plunder and pillage, traits of the brute.

That's what they said and more has to come
Like fighting for freedom, get rid of the scum,
Not long before the truth came to light
The scum were the ones that sent them to fight.

Stealing watches, gold teeth, and money
Killing the children then raping their mummy,
Soldiers together, all nazis and chummy
Denying their life then thinking it's funny.

Something has happened, cogs lost their grease
Squeaking in pain, a domino piece,
Touched by greed, first one to drop
Dragging them all, nothing to stop.

Hundreds of them, by thousands more
Lost their lives, it wasn't the war,
It was the thirst for blood and control
Finding it buried deep in a hole.

Imagine the world without all these fights
Without cruelty, violence and losses of lives,
A trillion humans, competing the flies
Not just in number but also in size.

It's a joke, really, the number of flies
The cruelty, competing, the violence and size,
The number of humans, it won't be that high
Try only ten dividing it by.

Heaven

Uncovered a new book of life
Reading through found love was rife,
A passage says, after you die
You will be waited with fresh pie.

Will be a Maybach and a Royce'
Virgins, models, it's your choice,
Homos, pans, bisexual
Lesbians, non-menstrual.

Everything tailored with care
Things you wish, they come in pair,
There is a catch to all this cite
You are accepted if you're white.

Suing left and suing right
Nobody left out of sight,
Any white is now a target
A 'me too' movement has just started.

They changed the text, from now is 'just blacks'
Number of virgins raised to max,
Maybachs, Royces swapped to Lambos
Delisted if you're fan of nachos.

Asians followed tout de suite
Starting with a stupid tweet,
We're coming over, take your virgins
Tax your meat and eat your vermin.

Finally, the rules were written
Buddhist style with blood of chicken,
Making voodoo intonations
Using Sumerian translations.

Pseudo

Square built, a large frame of a man
His face more like a failing plan,
No obvious signs of a brain
Rough DNA was to be blamed.

His eyelids usually in slumber
His unkempt hair slimy with blubber,
His nostrils showing off his nose
Less than a yard, you are too close.

She started laughing at his sight
Knowing was wrong and impolite,
She was a doctor as his shrink
Curvaceous body fitted pink.

Discernment wasn't his trait
Yet, knew she's laughing at his state,
He asked for window slight ajar
Pushed her through, a falling star.

The panegyric had his rhymes
A tribute read between the lines,
It said something about flying
Some kind of squeal, a shriek then dying.

The world had one less for a fraction
That was his only satisfaction,
As for justice? He was nuts,
That's why was acting like a klutz.

Hospice

Majestic view, a dark façade
Erected in spite of some god,
The image of a deathless force
Abode of life-ending source.

Gargoyles surveying the scene
Whoever's coming out or in,
Terror puncturing your spine
Death leaving behind its sign.

We found him hiding in a bed
His hope was gone, his soul was dead,
He asked for nothing but to see
The last two in his memory.

Who do you ask time to extend?
Who do you ask to try and mend?
The ugly god who gives the sentence?
The one who only wants repentance?

I suppose that's all's got left
But don't forget that you are blessed,
His stupid game to 'find the answer'
But he loves you, have some cancer!

CPSIA information can be obtained
at www.ICGtesting.com
Printed in the USA
BVHW052022200323
660800BV00002BA/31

9 781398 470149